Cycles of Nature

Migration

by Jaclyn Jaycox

Raintree is an imprint of Capstone Global Library Limited, a company incorporated in England and
Wales having its registered office at 264 Banbury Road, Oxford, OX2 7DY – Registered company
number: 6695582

www.raintree.co.uk
myorders@raintree.co.uk

Text and illustrations © Capstone Global Library Limited 2021
The moral rights of the proprietor have been asserted.

Editor: Alesha Sullivan
Designer: Charmaine Whitman
Media Researcher: Morgan Walters
Production Specialist: Katy LaVigne

ISBN 978 1 4747 9515 9 (hardback)
ISBN 978 1 4747 9527 2 (paperback)

British Library Cataloguing in Publication Data
A full catalogue record for this book is available from the British Library.

Acknowledgements
Capstone Press, (map) 11; Newscom: Thomas Kline, 13; Shutterstock: Alla Khananashvili, 5, Danita
Delmont, (butterflies) Cover, Ivan Hoermann, 7, JHVEPhoto, 9, John Wollwerth, 21, matthieu Gallet,
17, Paul Seftel, 15, Stacey Ann Alberts, (zebra) Cover, Tarcisio Schnaider, 19, Toluk, (circles) design
element throughout, Tory Kallman, (whale) Cover

Every effort has been made to contact copyright holders of material reproduced in this book. Any
omissions will be rectified in subsequent printings if notice is given to the publisher.

All the internet addresses (URLs) given in this book were valid at the time of going to press.
However, due to the dynamic nature of the internet, some addresses may have changed, or sites
may have changed or ceased to exist since publication. While the author and publisher regret any
inconvenience this may cause readers, no responsibility for any such changes can be accepted by
either the author or the publisher.

Printed in India
983

Contents

On the move

Some animals migrate for part of the year. They move to live in another place. Sometimes they travel very long distances. After several months, they return home.

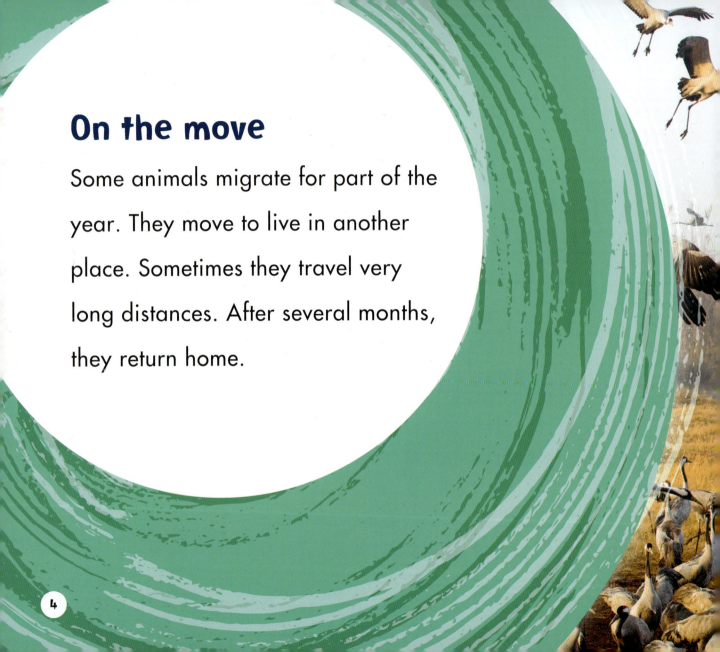

Grey cranes

Escaping the cold

Some animals live in places with very cold winters. They migrate to warmer places. These penguins travel for thousands of kilometres to find food and warmer weather.

Adélie penguins migrating

7

Monarch butterflies live in North America. They can't live in cold weather. They migrate south before the winter to find warmer weather until the spring. Many types of birds migrate south in the winter too.

Keeping babies safe

An animal's home might not be safe for babies. There may be too many animals that hunt them. Whales and sea turtles migrate to safer places to have their young.

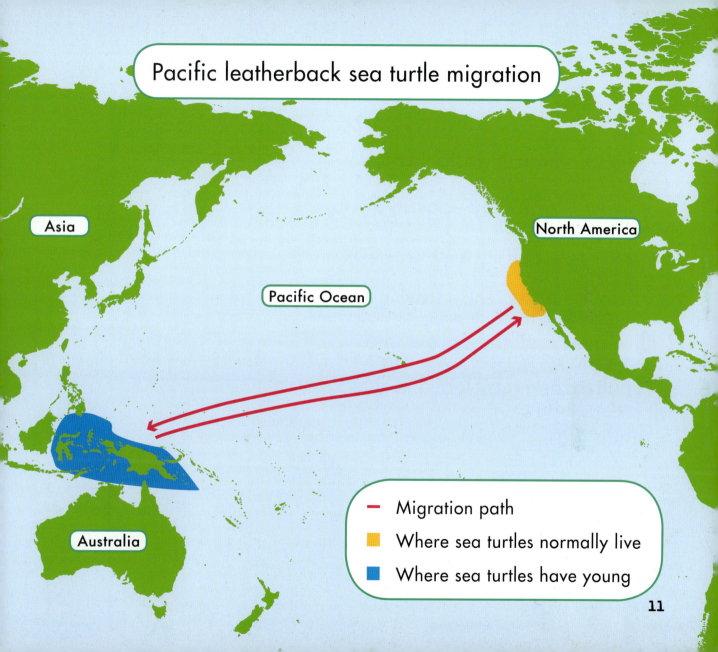

Pacific leatherback sea turtle migration

Asia

North America

Pacific Ocean

Australia

— Migration path

■ Where sea turtles normally live

■ Where sea turtles have young

11

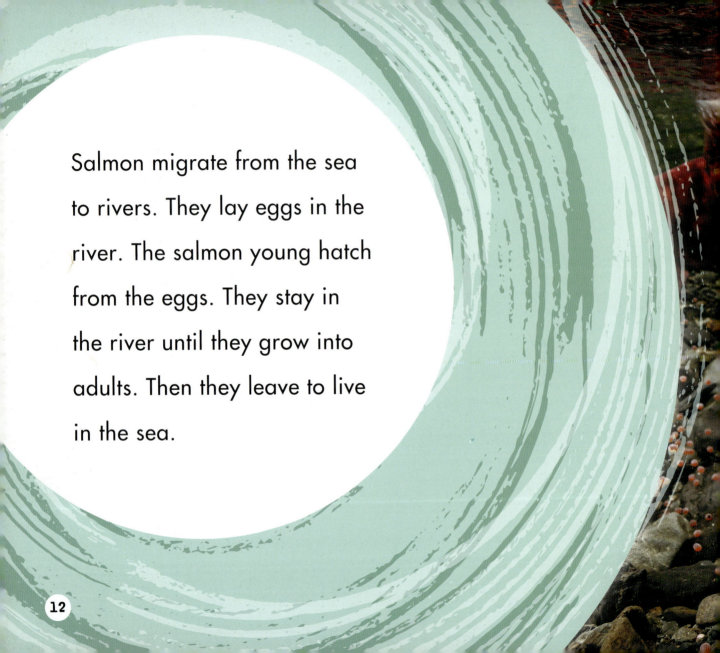

Salmon migrate from the sea to rivers. They lay eggs in the river. The salmon young hatch from the eggs. They stay in the river until they grow into adults. Then they leave to live in the sea.

Salmon eggs

Finding food

In places with cold winters, food can be hard to find. Other places have dry seasons. There is not enough water for animals to live there. Animals migrate to find food and water.

Elk

Zebras live in grasslands in Africa. They migrate during the dry season to find food and water.

Zebras

Humans and migration

People can change the way animals migrate. Forests are being cut down. Over time, pollution can cause the weather to change. This makes it difficult for some animals to migrate.

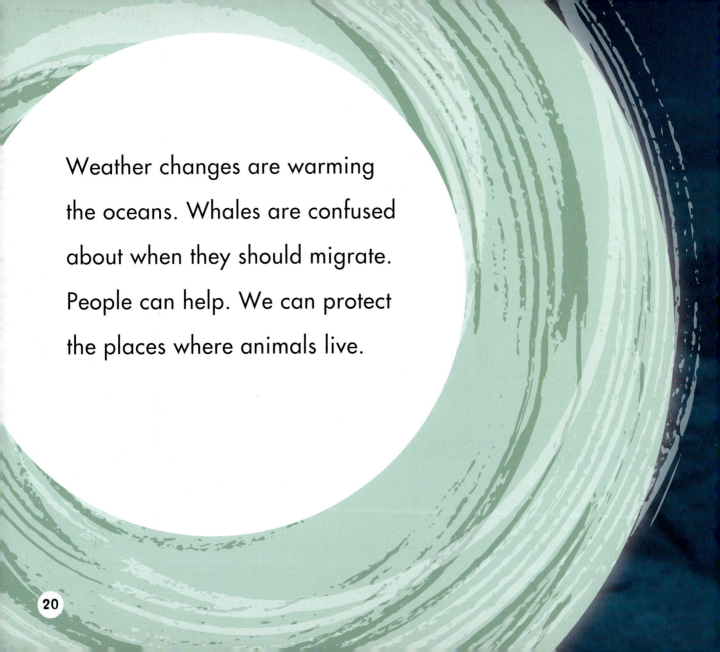

Weather changes are warming the oceans. Whales are confused about when they should migrate. People can help. We can protect the places where animals live.

Beluga whales

Comprehension questions

1. How do you think animals know when to migrate?

2. How else do you think humans affect migration?

3. What do you think could happen if an animal isn't able to migrate?

Index